Poems on Gender

by David Lee Morgan

Cover design by Richard Sharples

POEMS ON GENDER

GENDER IDENTITY

Everyone is at war with their gender
For some, it's a guerrilla warfare
For others, nuclear weapons at dawn
I guess you could say I was cis gender as a teen
I wanted to conform, I wanted to belong

Then women's liberation came to town
I had to be housetrained, of course
Learn to wash dishes and sweep the stairs
And as time went on, it would go deeper
I would learn things about myself
Things I had to change
But my first experience of women's liberation
Was as a liberation for me, too
I didn't have to be John Wayne anymore
(lucky thing, because I was shit at it)
Suddenly breaking gender rules was more than ok
It was cool – it was right on
Gay liberation intensified this
If you could be queer in front of the entire world
I could be brave too
And trans... one more giant fuck you
To the whole gender prison

We should be comrades
We should be allies
We should be friends
And we are
But friends can fall out

History is binary in terrible ways
Women have reason to fear men
Reason to fight for their own spaces, meetings, organisations
It's not self-determination that tears us apart – it's injustice

Now everything has changed – and nothing has
We are at the dawn of a new age of possibilities
But thousands of years of history
Do not go away with the stroke of a pen
The war goes on
We carry the enemy on our backs

Gender identity
Is not a home base
It's a prison
Or at best a day release
It's a compromise between
What we're expected to be
And what we could be

Gender identity
Is a war fought on the battleground of our bodies
There is an element of actual, real reality to it
We do, after all, have to reproduce, we have to make babies
(and raise them up so they can make more babies)
But for all the love that grows up out of this
The rules that are laid down on top of it
Are twisted through with power, property, ownership

Gender identity
Think of it as a brand
Like a game of cowboys
– where you are the cow
You're penned in
You try to escape
But they throw you down
Take the iron out of the fire
And burn it into your flesh
You fight your way free
But you carry the scars

And the scars become who you are
Your story, a record of all you have endured
All you have accomplished
A red badge of courage
And yours is not the only one
You realise now you are standing in a field of red
We are many
And we each have a story to tell

Sometimes rights intersect – sometimes they collide
History is binary in complicated ways
We don't all fit together like a finely crafted jigsaw puzzle
One love, one struggle, yes
But unity is not a god given state of grace
We have to fight for it
Fight to protect each other
Fight to understand each other
And sometimes, fight against each other
Not as enemies, but fearlessly
Like comrades, hungry for the truth
No matter how painful it is to learn

We are on the side of human liberation
We welcome debate
You have a right to be wrong
You have a right to make mistakes
We each have an obligation to be brave
To speak our mind
To dare to go against the tide
It's how we learn from each other
It's how we become strong
It's how we become kind

SUPPOSING

Supposing I thought of you as a man of courage
A man who knew his own mind
Who could look people in the eye and say
This is who I am
A man who could face danger for what he believes in
A man of commitment, down for the long haul
A man who could fight his own corner – and more
Someone you could count on to take your side
When you were facing injustice

Supposing I thought of you as a pioneer
We're only just ankle deep into this new frontier
But you've already jumped in
And you're swimming for the opposite shore

You tell me I can't be your friend
Unless I believe you are a real woman
I can't do that
We have our biology, like every other animal
Saying it isn't so doesn't make it go away
But gender is not biology, gender is a code
Gender is power, gender is control
And you are going up against it
How could I not respect that
How could I not fight alongside you
Just as I would any other comrade
How could I not rage at the bigotry you face

So much of human sexuality we don't think, only feel
Then the feelings think for us
From the pill to the knife to genetic engineering
What's going to be left of 'normal' in a hundred years?
The future is bright... and terrifying

Supposing I thought of you as a woman of courage
A woman who knew her own mind
Who could look people in the eye and say
This is who I am
A woman who could face danger for what she believes in
A woman of commitment, down for the long haul
A woman who could fight her own corner – and more
Someone you could count on to take your side
When you were facing injustice

Supposing I thought of you as a pioneer
We're only just ankle deep into this new frontier
But you've already jumped in
And you're swimming for the opposite shore

Supposing either way – what difference would it make?

GENDER ESSENTIALISM

There is no such thing as an essence of woman
There is no such thing as an essence of man
Not in biology
Not in gender identity
We don't exist as definitions
We exist as individuals
And even that is an abstraction
Where is it, exactly, that I end
And the rest of the universe begins?

The problem is...
History makes definitions
How does it do that?
By making victims

The definition of woman has been written in blood over thousands
of years
The definition of woman is a gaping wound in the heart of the
human race
The definition of woman is a fairy tale that began with the crack of a
whip
Because women are enslaved
Men are enslaved
Because women are enslaved
Children are property
Because women are enslaved
Sexuality is in chains
Deviation is a crime
Gender is a cage

How do you fight a definition?
First, you take over the prison
Then you burn down the walls

I am woman
Becomes a statement of power
You have given me a name
I will own it
And turn it into a weapon

I am woman
Becomes a battle cry
You have made us into an army
When we march
The earth will tremble

I am woman
Becomes a mighty fortress
But in a fortress, you are safe behind prison walls
Now is the time for fire
Burn down the walls, march out, and free the world

In the meantime
Before breakfast
Do the dishes from last night

One day there will be no such thing as woman or man
Only a rainbow
But the definition of woman is still being written today
The fortress still has walls, because they are still needed
After centuries of war, maybe the gatekeepers are edgy
But in a man's world, mistakes can be deadly
If you're knocking on the door, knock gently

TAKING SIDES

Can take you over
Can cloud your mind
Can make you forget
At first, you were fighting for a cause
Now you're just fighting to win

The devil can cite scripture for a purpose

Because they're the devil
They don't give a shit about the truth
You have to be made of sterner stuff
You have to be unbending about this
You are fighting for truth, nothing less
So you have to be fair
You have to take on their best arguments
Jumping on dumb mistakes might be amusing
Might be totally deserved
But you have to be constantly asking yourself
Why am I doing this
Is it to prove I was right
Or to get to the truth
And use it
To make a better world

There's a pure joy to be had
In tearing apart a hypocritical argument
It's fun to do and a great spectator sport
But don't pick at the edges
Don't go for the easy thrill
Go deep
Go to the heart of things
Cheap shots don't kill

BELIEVE SCIENTISTS

NO
No, no, no, no, no
Science is not a priesthood
It's not a College of Cardinals
No scientist, no matter how decorated
No matter how great their achievements
Is a Pope, speaking *ex cathedra*
Believe and obey
That's not science – that's religion
We don't need a planet of believers
We do need a planet of scientists

To respect science
You must become a scientist
You don't need a degree
You don't need a laboratory
You don't need a job working at the Hadron Collider
What you need, what we all need
Is a basic understanding of the scientific method
Of experimental design, the importance of sample size
Control groups, how to filter out the extraneous factors
How to read a scientific report with a bullshit detector

Science is not down to some mad genius in a basement
Writing equations on a blackboard that no one else understands
There is a place for that, but it's embedded in a vast social
enterprise
Modern science is a product of the printing press
And the telegraph and the telephone and the radio and the internet
Every advance in mass communication
Is a leap in our ability to learn from experience
Not just our own, but other people's too
That's what science is – a systematic way of doing this

Scientific knowledge is a social creation
And as long as society is a battleground
Between the rich and the poor
Science will be a battleground too
They say truth is the first casualty of war
But if you're fighting for a lie, you've already lost
So if you want to make a better world
If you're serious about revolution
If you want to be a soldier in the army of human liberation
You must become a scientist

TRANS PEOPLE IN PRISON

Prisons exist
To protect the rich
They have other functions too
But those are secondary
Collateral benefits, you might say
Or collateral damage

So first, about prisons
Tear them to the ground
Build new buildings
Start all over

Never gonna happen
Of course not
This is capitalism
There's money to be made
Power to be held onto

But let it be said
Before we start talking about band-aids
This is the swamp we live in
The pit we have to dig ourselves out of

Where should trans people be put
If they've broken the law
And they end up in prison
There is no correct answer
Only the least bad
This is a practical question
The guiding principle is love
Revolution is love, armed
Love, given power
Love, unleashed

But love is fighting in a world of ignorance and hate
Who is most likely to get raped?

You see how twisted the whole thing is
The answer should be nobody
Anywhere
Prisoners have a right to be protected
Women from men, the weak from the strong
The vulnerable, the disadvantaged
From sadistic guards and psychopaths
Prison should be safer than the street
And gender should be a festival, a rainbow
Even in prison, especially there

Imagine you're visiting another planet
They're showing you around
Showing off their world
You come to the last exhibit
The thing they're most proud of
They show you a prison
What?

This is how we judge other worlds, they say
The strong, the intelligent and brave
The loving and kind
We live in an almost paradise
We make the world and the world makes us
But the weak, the damaged, the dangerous
We make them too
If they're not safe
If they need to be locked away
That's not a judgement on them
It's a judgement on us
We haven't loved them enough

Show us your prisons
And we will tell you
What kind of world you live in

TWO SPIRIT

They gave us the Enlightenment
We thanked them with genocide
Their freedoms appalled the missionaries
But their ideas inspired Rousseau and Voltaire
The shoeless warriors of the Paris streets
When they stormed the Bastille
Were marching to a native beat

We killed them in the tens of millions
Cut down their forests
Slaughtered the animals
Salted the earth with slavery and disease
Now we come to pick over the bones
And use them as weapons
For our fashionable ideas

Two Spirit
Does not belong to us
It belongs to the cultures we destroyed
Over sixty thousand years of human history
Shattered, wisdom buried, wonders lost

I have read about cities, vast in scale
That rose up with a harvest moon
And then melted away in the spring

I have read that you could start
At the mouth of the Mississippi
Travel north to the Great Lakes
Through many tribes and villages
Many different languages
Many customs and traditions
And always find a welcome

I have read about the Turtle and the Bear
The Wolf, the Elk and the Beaver Clans
I have read that in some places, some times
If you had a dream
And it told you what to do
You had to do it
And anyone you met
If you told them about it
They had to help you out

We have glimpses of times and places
Where women and men were friends
Where both sexes were respected
Where the rules of gender
Had many variations
Many different meanings
And sometimes, maybe
Were not even rules at all

This was no lost paradise
It was life, blossom and thorn
There were wars, empires, slavery
Mistakes made, lessons learned
Revolutions of every kind

We have so many stories
Good and bad, terrible and surprising
But all just a tiny sliver of what was lost
Time and murder have done their work
There are only these last precious flowers
That survived into the modern world
From the land we slashed and burned

We can respect the flowers
We can be inspired by them
But we cannot copy them

We cannot own them
We cannot graft them onto the world we made
Onto the cancerous bones of class and sex and race
We cannot pretend ourselves out of the history we created

Leonard Peltier is dying in prison
Native women are still disappearing
The war against the land and its people
Goes on
The war against women
Goes on
The war against the poor
Goes on

We have no license to speak for those who survived
The genocide our ancestors brought with them
No license to spend their culture like easy money
To decorate the crimes and cruelties
Of a world we must destroy and build anew

First Peoples have a right to self-determination
The entire planet cries out for revolution
The war goes on – and we are losing
So tempting to crawl back into a land of fantasy
Where the personal is political and nothing else counts
But the war goes on – time is running out

It's good to learn from different cultures
Dangerous to imagine we understand what we don't
The past can be a magic mirror that shows us
Just exactly what we want to see
Or it can be an inspiration
All these things were possible
How many more?
What else can we do?

There are two sexes
Male and female
It takes one of each to make a baby
But what this means – what we make of it
Has changed more times than we can imagine
It will change in the future
It's changing now

If we are to choose the direction of that change
We must start with an honest look at the world we've made
Women have been oppressed by men through all of recorded
history
From the cities of the Nile and the Tigris and Euphrates
Down through the ages
Male supremacy
Embedded in the laws and institutions
Feeding into and fed by slavery, property, class war and violence
Gender is how they control us. Gender is how they divide us

Masculine and feminine are not different options
They're different forms of oppression
We need a repolarisation
Not the masculine and the feminine
But the good and the bad
The kind and the cruel
The brave and the cowardly
The rebel heart or the mind in slavery

MAKING BABIES

Imagine you're back in the Middle Ages in a room where a peasant woman is giving birth. She'd be in good company: the midwives, her mother, sisters, other women from the village...
Notice what's missing?

Capitalism, to keep on ticking, requires two things
One, making profits
Two, making babies
No profits without workers
No workers without babies
No babies without mothers
You can't make babies in a factory, yet
So to control the rate of reproduction
You have to control women's bodies

This is an old trick, an ancient trick
Goes way back as the beginning of class society
Capitalism didn't invent patriarchy
It took it over
And intensified it

It drove women out of the birthing room
Put men in charge
Brought in the death penalty
Not just for abortion – for contraception
A hundred thousand or more were burned as witches
Midwives were a big target
But mostly it was the aged, the homeless, the poor

The old feudal order was collapsing
Jacquerie, peasant rebellions
Were ripping across Europe
Heresy was a crime
You could die for it

But it kept rising up
Challenging the power of the Catholic church
Daring to dream of a heaven on earth
And ready to fight for it

Gunpowder was bad news for castle walls
Muskets were bad news for knightly armour
And the plague was bad news for everybody
Especially for the peasants, for the working poor
But as their numbers diminished, their power grew
Because they were necessary
Not just the work they did, but the land they occupied
They didn't own it, yet
But they'd worked it for hundreds of years
And kind of thought they should
Things were getting tough for the hard charging robber baron
There were banquets to be catered, wars to be fought
And even more wars as time went on
Because the slimmer the pickings, the more they scrapped over it

Meanwhile, trade was increasing
Manufacture had become a thing
Cities were getting richer, gaining independence
And they were hungry for bodies
But it was a new kind of body that was needed
Not tied to the land
Rootless
Something you could buy and sell
Move it around as necessary
Teach it to tell time by the clock not the sun
Discard when not needed

This was the rise of the nation state
The Kings, the Lords, the Church
All fighting against each other
But united against the poor

It was a match made in hell
Cities needed wool for the textile industry
The wool needed sheep, the sheep needed land
And the robber barons needed a new source of income
So the sheep ate the farms
The peasants were forced off the land
The Bloody Laws – that's what they were called
Made vagrancy a crime
Repeated vagrants got deportation or death
Men, women and children were driven into the factories
Into a poverty and degradation that made village life
With all its injustice and cruelty, look almost like paradise

And women were the biggest losers
Because only a woman could give birth
But it took a whole village to raise a child
Cooking, washing, spinning
These were all communal tasks
There was a power in this
But it was broken, when the people of the field
Were driven out of the commons and into a world
Where bodies on the job were paid by the hour
But making new bodies was a private affair
Hidden away, unpaid, disrespected

And right from the start, capitalism was a global disease
Witch burning was a pandemic on both sides of the ocean
Genocide in the Americas went hand in hand with the African slave
trade
Welcome to the Industrial Revolution, where human life is just
another commodity
Where they dump slaves into the ocean at the first sign of storm or
disease
Lloyds of London will cover the loss
And if you're a woman – and you survive the crossing
They don't just work you to death – they breed you like an animal

Making babies
From the hard cold point of view of evolution
Making babies is what life is all about
Love, this god-like emotion that binds us together
Grows up out of a simple biology
It's rooted in the core of what we are
In every gender, in every sexuality
The milk of human kindness
Imagine
To be a mother, to nurture
To carry a tiny bit of tissue
That grows, that multiplies, that complexifies
Until it comes out into the world as a new creation
A human individual
My god, what a gift, what a blessing it should be
And what a curse it is

The female body carries a double load
No matter how cruel we are to our fellow humans
Women get that little bit extra
Because they are nailed into their bodies
Not by any law of nature, but by man-made laws
In a capitalist world, witch-burning
Is the other side of motherhood

IF I HAD A HEART

What if Capitalism walked into a classroom and gave the students a
brief lecture entitled,
If I Had A Heart...

Okay, let's talk about the body
The body is a tool, but it's a product too
You have to buy your body back every day
Pay for the food you eat, the bed you sleep in
The clothes you wear, but even better, we can
Sell you a new body, a different colour hair
Shaved armpits, pubes, eyebrows, noses, piercings, tattoos
It's decoration, it's art, but we're just getting started
We can cut you into pieces and sew you back together
And let's be clear
This can be a wonderful thing to do
The body breaks down
And we can fix it, sometimes
And when we can't you die

But in the meantime, why stop at fixing it
Let's make a new body, yes we can
We're only at the starting stages
But the rocket's on the launch pad
And we can see the destination

Think of yourself as a grain of rice
Nature made you
And used to be, we just took what nature gave us
And thought up ways to make a buck out of it
But science happened, and now we own you
We have a copyright on your rice DNA
And we can go inside, chop it up, and glue it back together
Until nature can't do a damn thing unless we tell it to

The human personality is an infinite onion
You can peel away the skin, layer by layer
And never get to the bottom
The inside goes on forever
But the human body is not like that
It's like a grain of rice
More complicated, same principle
We can map it
And then make you buy back every damn inch of it

If I had a heart, I would pity you
We start fucking with your head before you're even born

TRANSITION

(trigger warning)

Some things hurt so bad you have to cut them out
You have to be like a soldier
Who digs a bullet out of their own flesh
Pinches the wound together
And marches on

Was it like that for you

If I had loved you better
If I had loved you more
You would have been stronger
Would that have made a difference
I don't know

They told me you would kill yourself

My child was a beautiful baby
My baby is a beautiful child
A rainbow
One of a kind

This is what I believe
You came for my child
You took a rainbow and forged it into a knife
You were nothing but a hammer looking for a nail
How could you not understand that a rainbow
Is not a problem to be solved
It's a rainbow

Did you wound my child or heal them
How can we ever know

You stormed in like a Jesuit missionary
Waving a holy book as if it were a sword of truth

Listen to the children you say
But you don't know what listening is
It's engagement, it's giving back
Love is struggle – not war, but not surrender
You never give up on each other

My child was a beautiful baby
My baby is a beautiful child
A rebel spirit
A revolutionary

This is what I believe
The body is the foundation
When the body dies, the music stops
Physical transition comes with a lifelong cost
So of course you would try to avoid it
Not at any price
But that's where you would start
How could you not understand this

We all sing the body electric
We all sing out of tune
Perfect harmony is boring
Rules have teeth
Rules have claws
But even the harshest rules
Make a beautiful sound
When they're broken

We should break rules
Not bodies
Bodies are a fact
We give them meaning

We build on them
We can make whole castles
Out of fairy tales and logic
But the fact remains

My child was a beautiful baby
My baby is a beautiful child
Always and forever

NAILING THE SOUL BACK INTO THE BODY

One nail at a time
Or taken all altogether
The nails tell a story
The story is a lie
You are not the colour of your skin
The sex of your body
Or the calluses on your hand
You are a blossom
Rooted in the earth
Soaking up the sunlight
Of a hundred billion stars

When I was a kid
We were nailed into our bodies
There were things a man could do
That a woman never could
There were places white could go
Where black would never be allowed
And always, there was the enemy
Foreign bodies, just across the border
Across the ocean
Across the wrong side of the tracks

Vietnam
Blew my mind
The Vietnamese people were fighting off
The most powerful imperialist army
In the history of the world
My country, my army
But they were the freedom fighters
We were the invaders
Truth, Justice, and the American Way
– all my life I had believed this lie
Now everything changed

As I looked at the world
Through Vietnamese eyes

Bring The War Home, we chanted
And the war came home
Not as a curse, but a gift
As an invitation
Join us
And we did

Revolution
Was like stepping into a different dimension
Everything was turned inside out
Two, three, many Vietnams
Asia, Africa, Latin America
Home of the Brave, Land of the Free
Bad was good
And what I had thought was good was
Monstrous
Imperialism
I had never even heard that word
– outside of a sword and toga movie
But once you start digging up bodies
You find them buried everywhere

Bring The War Home, we chanted
And now I could see
The war was already here
I could see freedom fighters on every corner
And I could see the enemy too
We carried the enemy on our backs
Nailed into our bodies

What is the human soul but the body unleashed
The body set free
The body in all its mystery and secret

In all its possibilities
In all its interconnectedness
I am not as strong as the tiger
I cannot swim like a fish
Or fly in the air like a bird
What makes me unique
Is you
I speak your words
I sing your melodies
I dance to the music of you

Freedom is not some king on a mountaintop
Master of all he surveys, beholden to none
Freedom is you, your body
In all its frailty and power
Hopes and fears
Hunger and thirst
Freedom is you and I
Feeding each other
Food for the stomach
Courage for the heart
Ideas for the imagination

How can it be
That we slaughter each other
For an algorithm, a parasite
An invisible god that rules over the planet
With one law, one commandment, make money
More money, more money, more money
Grow or die
And all our achievements
All of the wonders we create
Are grabbed hold of and twisted
Into a machine for murder
A hammer to smash the earth
A knife to cut into our own hearts

Race, nation, gender, class
These things do not exist inside our bodies
They do not belong to us, we belong to them
It's how we are nailed into the machine
How we becomes its movable parts

And of all these, gender is primal
It attacks what we are
On the deepest level of our biology
Sex is the body, the human animal
Gender is capitalism, trying to ride the tiger
Gender is the spur and the whip
And you can't get away from it
You can't have no gender
— anymore than you can speak without an accent
It's a gendered world — thems are the rules
And either you break'em or you don't
But whatever you choose
You are punching in a bar code

Gender abolition — as if we could
Gender is a nail that gets pounded into each of us
Day in, day out, cradle to grave
Gender Identity
Is the scar tissue that forms around the nail
As the body tries to heal itself
But it can't heal
Because the nail is still there
And it's not going away
Because the problem is not just the nail
The problem is the hammer
That keeps pounding it in

Learn to love the nail
Does not work

Because if you don't push back
It just goes in deeper
So you gotta keep on pushing back
Forever
Or else you gotta get to the hammer
And get rid of it
Not change it
Not make it nicer
Not give it a shiny new handle
Get rid of it
Unleash the body
Liberate the soul
And free the world

IN PRAISE OF KINK – THE ETHICS OF DREAM

Don't get suckered into becoming
A puritanical, carrot-up-the-ass, gender fascist
Sexuality is fucking complicated
Pain can damage, but it can also heal
A fantasy can be fun, it can be an adventure, it can be a therapy, it
can be an exorcism
Or it can dig deeper into the wound, rub disease into it, and infect
the soul
What turns you on is not – never should be – a cause for shame
The question is what you do with it
Do you harm other people
Do you harm yourself

I read a story about a faraway tribe
Who had no rules for how to behave
When they were awake
Instead, they had an ethics of dream
Every morning at breakfast
They would talk about the night's adventures
What they had done
What they could have done differently
They were guided by a few basic principles
Whenever you meet someone
You should greet them in a friendly fashion
But if they attack you, you must fight back
If somebody kills you in a dream
Don't wake up
Stay
And be reborn in a stronger form
And always
The last thing you do
No matter what's happened
When you say goodbye
Ask them for a gift

Printed in Great Britain
by Amazon